All rights Reserved. No part of this publication or the information in it may be quoted from or reproduced in any form by means such as printing, scanning, photocopying or otherwise without prior written permission of the copyright holder.

Disclaimer and Terms of Use: Effort has been made to ensure that the information in this book is accurate and complete, however, the author and the publisher do not warrant the accuracy of the information, text and graphics contained within the book due to the rapidly changing nature of science, research, known and unknown facts and internet. The Author and the publisher do not hold any responsibility for errors, omissions or contrary interpretation of the subject matter herein. This book is presented solely for motivational and informational purposes only.

CONTENTS

What are Keto Cookies?	3
What are the Key Differentiators?	4
What are the Key Ingredients?	5
What Ingredients can't be used in Keto Cookies?	6
Keto Cookie Recipes	7
Vanilla Cookies	8
Almond Cookies	10
Shortbread Cookies	12
Peanut Butter Cookies	14
Spiced Butter Cookies	16
Cinnamon Cookies	18
Cinnamon Swirl Cookies	20
Star Cookies	22
Crescent Cookies	24
Gingerbread Men Cookies	26
Gingersnap Cookies	28
Carrot Cake Cookies	30
Orange Cranberry Cookies	32
Lemon Cookies	34
Chocolate Bacon Cookies	36
Chocolate Cookies	38
Double Chocolate Cookies	40
Chocolate Kiss Cookies	42
Thumbprint Cookies	44
Meringue Cookies	46
Cream Cheese Cookies	48
Cream Cheese Pumpkin Cookies	50
Orange Cream Cheese Cookies	52
Chocolate Sandwich Cookies	54
Pumpkin Sandwich Cookies	56

INTRODUCTION

WHAT ARE KETO COOKIES?

The keto cookies are the most popular choice when it comes to keto snacks or desserts amongst the keto followers. The low-carb cookies are the best recipe that can be easily prepared in no time. They are very simple and can be made easily by using key alternatives for specific ingredients. These alterations are basically keto friendly and thus makes the cookies 'keto.' The sugar-free cookies are a better option for having them for snacks on a keto diet plan because they have a high quantity of butter in them, thus your fat intake is high; always opt for a butter of high quality or any other similar nut butter.

Irrespective of its name, be it low-carb cookies, almond flour cookies, almond meal cookies, or even keto cookies, they are usually the same as they belong to the same family of foods. And assist each other out like other keto diet-oriented foods.

WHAT ARE THE KEY DIFFERENTIATORS?

The keto cookies are similar to the usual recipe of cookies apart from some pivotal amendments in the ingredients, which basically makes the cookies keto friendly for you. Following amendments to regular cookie recipes are useful in making your cookies keto friendly and low carb in nature:

- The flour can be replaced with coconut flour or almond flour.
- Replace the sugar to avoid increasing your blood glucose levels by using keto-friendly sweeteners like Erythritol, Swerve, Xylitol, or Natvia, etc.

WHAT ARE THE KEY INGREDIENTS?

There are many keto ingredients that can be tried together to prepare keto cookies, like the following:

- Fats like butter, coconut oil, etc.
- Sweeteners like stevia, Natvia, Xylitol, Swerve, Erythritol, monk fruit, and Yacon syrup, etc.
- Flours like almond flour, coconut flour, etc.
- Butter, cheeses, cream cheese, cream, etc.
- Non-dairy milk like coconut milk and almond milk

WHAT INGRE- DIENTS CAN'T BE USED IN KETO COOKIES?

Non-keto ingredients aren't allowed for prepping your keto recipes, and these include the following ingredients:

- Sugar-rich ingredients like honey, aspartame, maple syrup, etc.
- Grain or their derived flours like wheat, etc.

KETO COOKIE RECIPES

VANILLA COOKIES

YIELD:

18 Servings

PREPARATION TIME:

15 Minutes

COOKING TIME:

12 Minutes

INGREDIENTS:
- 1/2 cup Erythritol
- 1/3 cup butter, softened
- 1 teaspoon organic vanilla extract
- 2 1/2 cups almond flour

DIRECTIONS:
1. Preheat the oven to 350 degrees F. Line a large cookie sheet with parchment paper.
2. In a bowl, add the Erythritol and butter and beat until fluffy.
3. Add the vanilla extract and beat until well blended.
4. Slowly, add the flour, 1/2 cup at a time, and mix until a sticky dough forms.
5. With a round tablespoon, place the cookies onto the prepared cookie sheet in a single layer about two inches apart.
6. With your palm, flatten each cookie into 1/3-inch thickness.
7. Bake for about 12 minutes.
8. Remove from the oven and place onto a wire rack to cool in the pan for about 5-10 minutes.
9. Carefully, invert the cookies onto the wire rack to cool completely before serving.

NUTRITION INFORMATION PER SERVING:

Calories: 120

Fat: 11.2g

Carbohydrates: 3.4g

Protein: 3.4g

ALMOND COOKIES

YIELD: 20 Servings

PREPARATION TIME: 15 Minutes

COOKING TIME: 10 Minutes

NUTRITION INFORMATION PER SERVING:

Calories: 107

Fat: 8.9g

Carbohydrates: 5.8g

Protein: 4.1g

INGREDIENTS:
- 2 cups super-fine almond flour
- 1/4 cup unsweetened whey protein powder
- 5 teaspoons Swerve
- 1 teaspoon organic baking powder
- 3 teaspoons gingerbread spice
- 1 large organic egg (white and yolk separated)
- 1/4 cup Yacon syrup
- 1/4 cup butter, melted
- 1 tablespoon unsweetened almond milk
- 20 whole almonds

DIRECTIONS:
1. In a large bowl, add the almond flour, protein powder, Swerve, baking powder, and gingerbread spice and mix well.
2. In another bowl, add the egg white, Yacon syrup, and butter and beat until well combined.
3. Add the butter mixture into the bowl of the flour mixture and mix until well combined.
4. Refrigerate for about 30 minutes.
5. Preheat oven to 350 degrees F. Line two large cookie sheets with parchment paper.
6. Remove the dough from refrigerator and arrange between two wax paper sheets.
7. With a rolling pin, roll the dough into 1/8-inch thickness.
8. With a cookie cutter, cut the cookies and arrange onto the prepared cookie sheets in a single layer about two inches apart.

9. In a bowl, add the almond milk and egg yolk and beat slightly.
10. Coat the top of the cookie with the almond milk mixture.
11. Place an almond in the center of each cookie and gently press it.
12. Bake for about 8-10 minutes or until the edges become golden brown.
13. Remove from the oven and place onto a wire rack to cool in the pan for about 5-10 minutes.
14. Carefully, invert the cookies onto the wire rack to cool completely before serving.

SHORTBREAD COOKIES

YIELD:

18 Servings

PREPARATION TIME:

15 Minutes

COOKING TIME:

12 Minutes

INGREDIENTS:
- 1/2 cup powdered stevia
- 6 tablespoons butter, softened
- 1 teaspoon organic vanilla extract
- 2 1/2 cups almond flour

DIRECTIONS:
1. Preheat the oven to 350 degrees F. Line a large cookie sheet with parchment paper.
2. In a bowl, add the stevia and butter and beat until light and fluffy.
3. Add the vanilla extract and beat until well combined.
4. Slowly, add the flour, one cup at a time and mix until a sticky dough forms.
5. Arrange the dough between two wax paper sheets and with a rolling pin, roll the dough into 1/3-inch thickness.
6. With a heart-shaped cookie cutter, cut the cookies.
7. Place the cookies onto the prepared cookie sheet in a single layer about two inches apart.
8. Bake for about 12 minutes or until edges become golden brown.
9. Remove from the oven and place onto a wire rack to cool in the pan for about 5-10 minutes.
10. Carefully, invert the cookies onto the wire rack to cool completely before serving.

NUTRITION INFORMATION PER SERVING:

Calories: 123

Fat: 11.6g

Carbohydrates: 3.4g

Protein: 3.4g

PEANUT BUTTER COOKIES

YIELD:

24 Servings

PREPARATION TIME:

20 Minutes

COOKING TIME:

17 Minutes

NUTRITION INFORMATION PER SERVING:

Calories: 73

Fat: 6g

Carbohydrates: 2.4g

Protein: 3.4g

INGREDIENTS:
- 1/2 cup coconut flour
- 1 cup creamy peanut butter
- 1 cup granulated sucralose
- 3 organic eggs
- 1 teaspoon organic vanilla extract
- 1/4 teaspoon salt

DIRECTIONS:
1. Preheat the oven to 350 degrees F. Line a large cookie sheet with parchment paper.
2. In the bowl of an electric mixer, add all of ingredients and mix until a dough forms.
3. With a tablespoon, place the cookies onto the prepared cookie sheet in a single layer about two inches apart.
4. With a fork, flatten each cookie slightly to make a crisscross mark.
5. Bake for about 15-17 minutes or until the edges become golden brown.
6. Remove from the oven and place onto a wire rack to cool in the pan for about 5-10 minutes.
7. Carefully, invert the cookies onto the wire rack to cool completely before serving.

YIELD:

40 Servings

PREPARATION TIME:

20 Minutes

COOKING TIME:

12 Minutes

NUTRITION INFORMATION PER SERVING:

Calories: 60

Fat: 5.5g

Carbohydrates: 1.7g

Protein: 1.9g

SPICED BUTTER COOKIES

INGREDIENTS:
- 2 cups almond flour
- 2 tablespoons grass-fed gelatin
- 1/2 teaspoon baking soda
- 1 tablespoon ground ginger
- 1 teaspoon ground cinnamon
- 1 cup Swerve Sweetener
- 1/2 cup almond butter
- 1/2 cup butter, softened
- 2 large organic eggs
- 2 teaspoons Yacon syrup
- 1/4 teaspoon organic vanilla extract

DIRECTIONS:
1. Preheat the oven to 325 degrees F. Line two baking sheets with parchment paper.
2. In a bowl, add the almond flour, gelatin, baking soda, ginger, and cinnamon and mix well.
3. In another large bowl, add the remaining ingredients and beat until smooth.
4. Add the flour mixture and beat until a dough forms.
5. Make about one-inch balls from the dough.
6. Place the cookies onto the prepared cookie sheet in a single layer about two inches apart.
7. Bake for about 5 minutes.

8. Remove the cookie sheet from the oven and with a fork, press down each ball.
9. Bake or about 7 minutes or until the edges become golden brown.
10. Remove from the oven and place onto a wire rack to cool in the pan for about 5-10 minutes.
11. Carefully invert the cookies onto the wire rack

CINNAMON COOKIES

YIELD:

PREPARATION TIME:

COOKING TIME:

NUTRITION INFORMATION PER SERVING:

Calories: 133

Fat: 12.8g

Carbohydrates: 2.9g

Protein: 3.1g

INGREDIENTS:
- 2 cups almond meal
- 1 teaspoon ground cinnamon
- 1 organic egg
- 1/2 cup salted butter, softened
- 1 teaspoon liquid stevia
- 1 teaspoon organic vanilla extract

DIRECTIONS:
1. Preheat the oven to 300 degrees F. Grease a large cookie sheet.
2. In a large bowl, add all of the ingredients and mix until well combined.
3. Make fifteen equal-sized balls.
4. Arrange the balls onto the prepared baking sheet in a single layer about two inches apart.
5. Bake for about 5 minutes.
6. Remove the cookie sheet from the oven and with a fork press down each ball.
7. Bake or about 18-20 minutes or until the edges become golden brown.
8. Remove from the oven and place onto the wire rack to cool in the pan for about 5-10 minutes.
9. Carefully, invert the cookies onto the wire rack to cool completely before serving.

CINNAMON SWIRL COOKIES

YIELD:

20 Servings

PREPARATION TIME:

20 Minutes

COOKING TIME:

30 Minutes

NUTRITION INFORMATION PER SERVING:

Calories: 112

Fat: 9.8g

Carbohydrates: 4.5g

Protein: 4g

INGREDIENTS:
- 3 cups almond flour
- 1/2 cup powdered Swerve
- 2 teaspoons organic baking powder
- 1/4 teaspoon salt
- 2 tablespoons butter
- 1 large organic egg
- 2 tablespoons ground cinnamon

DIRECTIONS:
1. In a bowl, add the almond flour, Swerve, baking powder, and salt and mix well.
2. Add the butter and egg and with your hands and mix well
3. Divide the dough into two equal-sized portions.
4. Add cinnamon into one portion and with your hands mix well.
5. In a bowl, place both dough portions.
6. With plastic wrap, cover the bowl and refrigerate for about 30 minutes.
7. Preheat the oven to 280 degrees F. Line a large cookie sheet with parchment paper.
8. Remove the bowl from refrigerator and arrange the plain dough between two wax paper sheets.

9. With a rolling pin, roll the dough into 1/4-inch thickness.
10. Now, place the cinnamon dough between two wax paper sheets and with a rolling pin, roll the dough into 1/2-inch thickness.
11. Arrange the cinnamon dough on top of the plain dough.
12. With your hands, roll the dough up tightly and carefully fold the edges.
13. With a sharp knife, cut the dough into 1/2-inch thick slices.
14. With your fingers, gently press down each cookie to flatten.
11. Arrange the cookies onto the prepared cookie sheet, pressed side down into a single layer about two inches apart.
12. Bake for about 25-30 minutes or until the edges become golden brown.
13. Remove from the oven and place onto a wire rack to cool in the pan for about 5-10 minutes.
14. Carefully, invert the cookies onto the wire rack to cool completely before serving.

STAR COOKIES

YIELD:

32 Servings

PREPARATION TIME:

15 Minutes

COOKING TIME:

8 Minutes

NUTRITION INFORMATION PER SERVING:

Calories: 69

Fat: 6.1g

Carbohydrates: 3.7g

Protein: 1.1g

INGREDIENTS:
- 2 1/2 cups blanched almond flour
- 1/4 teaspoon baking soda
- 1 teaspoon ground cinnamon
- 1/2 teaspoon salt
- 1/4 cup coconut oil, melted
- 5 tablespoons Yacon syrup
- 1 tablespoon organic vanilla extract

DIRECTIONS:
1. In a large bowl, add the almond flour, baking soda, cinnamon, and salt and mix well.
2. Add the remaining ingredients and mix until well combined.
3. Arrange the dough between two wax paper sheets.
4. With a rolling pin, roll the dough into 1/4-inch thickness.
5. Refrigerate the rolled dough for about 1 hour.
6. Preheat the oven to 350 degrees F. Line a large cookie sheet with parchment paper.
7. Remove from the refrigerator, and with a star-shaped cookie cutter, cut the cookies.
8. Place the cookies onto the prepared cookie sheet in a single layer about two inches apart.
9. Bake for about 5-8 minutes or until the edges become golden brown.
10. Remove from the oven and place onto a wire rack to cool in the pan for about 5-10 minutes.
11. Carefully, invert the cookies onto the wire rack to cool completely before serving.

CRESCENT COOKIES

YIELD:

24 Servings

PREPARATION TIME:

20 Minutes

COOKING TIME:

15 Minutes

NUTRITION INFORMATION PER SERVING:

Calories: 201

Fat: 18.5g

Carbohydrates: 6.9g

Protein: 4.7g

INGREDIENTS:
- 1 1/4 cups Xylitol
- 1 cup butter, softened
- 1/4 teaspoon salt
- 1 1/2 teaspoons organic almond extract
- 1 teaspoon organic vanilla extract
- 3 3/4 cups almond flour
- 1/2 cup coconut flour
- 1 cup sliced almonds
- 1/4 cup powdered Swerve sweetener

DIRECTIONS:
1. Preheat the oven to 350 degrees F. Lightly, grease two cookie sheets.
2. In a bowl, add the Xylitol, butter, and salt and beat until well combined.
3. Add both extracts and beat well.
4. Add flours and mix until well combined.
5. Make three-inch long, small logs from the dough.
6. In a shallow dish, place in the sliced almonds.
7. Coat the dough logs with the sliced almonds, and carefully, shape each into a crescent.
8. Place the cookies onto the prepared cookie sheets in a single layer and sprinkle with Swerve.

9. Bake for about 10-15 minutes or until the edges become golden brown.
10. Remove from the oven and place onto a wire rack to cool in the pan for about 5-10 minutes.
11. Carefully, invert the cookies onto the wire rack to cool completely before serving.
12. Dust the cookies with powdered Swerve generously and serve.

GINGERBREAD MEN COOKIES

YIELD:

40 Servings

PREPARATION TIME:

20 Minutes

COOKING TIME:

10 Minutes

NUTRITION INFORMATION PER SERVING:

Calories: 51

Fat: 4.4g

Carbohydrates: 2g

Protein: 1.5g

INGREDIENTS:
- 2 cups almond flour
- 2 tablespoons coconut flour
- 1/2 cup powdered Swerve sweetener
- 1/2 teaspoon baking powder
- 1 tablespoon ground ginger
- 1 tablespoon ground cinnamon
- 1/2 tablespoon ground nutmeg
- Pinch of salt
- 1 large organic egg
- 1/4 cup butter, melted
- 2 tablespoons cream cheese, softened
- 1 teaspoon organic vanilla extract

DIRECTIONS:
1. In a bowl, add the flours, Swerve, baking powder, spices, and salt and mix well.
2. Add the remaining ingredients and mix until a dough forms.
3. With plastic wrap, wrap the dough and refrigerate for about 2-3 hours.
4. Preheat the oven to 350 degrees F. Line two large cookie sheets with parchment paper.
5. Remove the dough from refrigerator and arrange between two wax paper sheets.
6. With a rolling pin, roll the dough into 1/4-inch thickness.

7. With a cookie cutter, cut the cookies into man shape.
8. Arrange the cookies onto the prepared cookie sheets in a single layer about two inches apart.
9. Bake for about 8-10 minutes or until the edges become golden brown.
10. Remove from the oven and place onto a wire rack to cool in the pan for about 5-10 minutes.
11. Carefully, invert the cookies onto the wire rack to cool completely before serving.
12. Decorate the cookies with keto friendly icing and food safe markers.

GINGER-SNAP COOKIES

YIELD:

24 Servings

PREPARATION TIME:

20 Minutes

COOKING TIME:

18 Minutes

NUTRITION INFORMATION PER SERVING:

Calories: 147

Fat: 14.3g

Carbohydrates: 3.3g

Protein: 3.5g

INGREDIENTS:
- 3 cups almond flour
- 1 cup Erythritol
- 1/2 teaspoon baking soda
- 1/4 teaspoon cream of tartar
- 1 tablespoon ground ginger
- 1/2 teaspoon ground cinnamon
- 1/4 teaspoon ground cloves
- 1/4 teaspoon ground nutmeg
- 1/4 teaspoon salt
- 1/2 cup butter
- 1/3 cup coconut oil
- 2 organic eggs
- 1 teaspoon organic vanilla extract

DIRECTIONS:
1. Preheat the oven to 350 degrees F. Line two baking sheets with parchment paper.
2. In a bowl, add the almond flour, Erythritol, baking soda, cream of tartar, spices, and salt and mix well.
3. In another bowl, add the butter and coconut oil, and with a hand mixer, beat until well combined.
4. Add the eggs and vanilla extract and beat until well combined.
5. Add the flour mixture and mix until well combined.

6. Make small, equal-sized balls from the dough and place them onto the prepared cookie sheets in a single layer about four inches apart.
7. With your palm, flatten each ball slightly.
8. Bake for about 15-18 minutes or until the edges become golden brown.
9. Remove from the oven and place onto a wire rack to cool in the pan for about 5-10 minutes.
10. Carefully, invert the cookies onto the wire rack to cool completely before serving.

CARROT CAKE COOKIES

YIELD:

12 Servings

PREPARATION TIME:

20 Minutes

COOKING TIME:

14 Minutes

NUTRITION INFORMATION PER SERVING:

Calories: 147

Fat: 14.3g

Carbohydrates: 3.3g

Protein: 3.5g

INGREDIENTS:
- 3/4 cup almond flour
- 1/4 cup coconut flour
- 1/4 teaspoon baking soda
- 1/4 teaspoon salt
- 1 large organic egg
- 3/4 cup Erythritol
- 4 tablespoons butter, melted
- 1 teaspoon organic vanilla extract
- 1/3 cup chopped walnuts
- 1/4 cup peeled, shredded, and chopped carrots

DIRECTIONS:
1. Preheat the oven to 350 degrees F. Line a large cookie sheet with parchment paper.
2. In a bowl, add the flours, baking soda, and salt and mix well.
3. In another large bowl, add the egg, Erythritol, butter, and vanilla extract and beat until well combined.
4. Add the flour mixture and mix until a dough forms.
5. Gently, fold in the walnuts and carrots.
6. With a one-inch cookie scooper, scoop twelve cookies onto the prepared cookie sheets in a single layer about four inches apart.

7. With your palm, flatten each cookie slightly.
8. Bake for about 12-14 minutes or until the edges become golden brown.

Remove from the oven and place onto a wire rack to cool in the pan for about 5-10 minutes.

Carefully, invert the cookies onto the wire rack to cool completely before serving.

ORANGE CRANBERRY COOKIES

YIELD:

36 Servings

PREPARATION TIME:

20 Minutes

COOKING TIME:

10 Minutes

INGREDIENTS:
- 1/2 cup coconut flour
- 1 1/2 teaspoons organic baking powder
- 1/4 teaspoon baking soda
- 3 organic eggs
- 3/4 cup butter, softened
- 3/4 cup Swerve sweetener
- 1/2 cup chopped walnuts
- 1/4 cup sugar-free dried cranberries
- 1 1/2 teaspoons grated orange zest

DIRECTIONS:
1. Preheat the oven to 350 degrees F. Line a large cookie sheet with parchment paper.
2. In a bowl, add the flour, baking powder, and baking soda and mix well.
3. In another large bowl, add eggs, butter, and Swerve, and with an electric mixer, beat until well combined.
4. Add the flour mixture and beat on low speed until well combined.
5. Add the walnuts, cranberries, and orange zest and gently stir to combine.
6. With a cookie scoop, place the cookies onto the prepared cookie sheet in a single layer about one inch apart.

NUTRITION INFORMATION PER SERVING:

Calories: 52

Fat: 3.5g

Carbohydrates: 0.5g

Protein: 1g

7. With your palm, flatten each cookie slightly.
8. Bake for about 8-10 minutes or until edges become golden brown.
9. Remove from the oven and place onto a wire rack to cool in the pan for about 5-10 minutes.
10. Carefully, invert the cookies onto the wire rack to cool completely before serving.

LEMON COOKIES

YIELD:

6 Servings

PREPARATION TIME:

20 Minutes

COOKING TIME:

10 Minutes

NUTRITION INFORMATION PER SERVING:

Calories: 196

Fat: 16.6g

Carbohydrates: 10g

Protein: 5g

INGREDIENTS:
FOR COOKIES:
- 3/4 cup super-fine almond flour
- 1 tablespoon coconut flour
- 1/2 teaspoon xanthan gum
- 1/2 teaspoon organic baking powder
- 1/4 teaspoon salt
- 1/3 cup Swerve
- 1/4 cup butter, softened
- 1 large organic egg
- 1 large organic egg yolk
- 1 tablespoon fresh lemon juice
- 1 teaspoon freshly grated lemon zest
- 1 teaspoon organic vanilla extract

FOR ICING:
- 8 tablespoons powdered Swerve
- 2 tablespoons fresh lemon juice

DIRECTIONS:
1. Preheat the oven to 350 degrees F. Line a large cookie sheet with parchment paper.
2. For cookies: in a bowl, sift together the flours, xanthan gum, baking powder, and salt.
3. In another bowl, add the Swerve and butter, and with an electric hand mixer, beat until creamy.

4. Add the egg, egg yolk, lemon juice, zest, and vanilla extract and beat until well combined.
5. Slowly, add the flour mixture, beating continuously until well combined.
6. Make six equal-sized balls from the mixture, and with your hands, flatten each into 1/3-inch thickness.
7. Place the cookies onto the prepared cookie sheet in a single layer about two inches apart.
8. Bake for about 8-10 minutes or until edges become golden brown.
9. Remove from the oven and place onto a wire rack to cool in the pan for about 5-10 minutes.
10. Carefully, invert the cookies onto the wire rack to cool completely before icing.
11. Meanwhile, for icing: in a bowl, add the powdered Swerve and lemon juice and mix until desired consistency is achieved.
12. Spread the icing over the cookies and serve.

CHOCOLATE BACON COOKIES

YIELD:

30 Servings

PREPARATION TIME:

25 Minutes

COOKING TIME:

35 Minutes

INGREDIENTS:
- 5 bacon slices
- 3/4 cup Yacon syrup, divided
- 3 cups blanched almond flour
- 1 teaspoon baking soda
- 1 teaspoon salt
- 1/2 cup coconut oil, melted
- 2 organic eggs
- 1 teaspoon organic vanilla extract
- 1 1/2 cups 70% dark chocolate chips

DIRECTIONS:
1. Preheat the oven to 350 degrees F. Line a large baking sheet with parchment paper.
2. In a bowl, add bacon and 1/4 cup of Yacon syrup and toss to coat well.
3. Arrange the bacon slices onto the prepared baking sheet in a single layer.
4. Bake for about 20 minutes.
5. Remove from the oven and transfer the bacon onto a paper towel-lined plate to cool.
6. Then, crumble the candied bacon.
7. Preheat the oven from 350 degrees to 375 degrees F. Line a large cookie sheet with parchment paper.

NUTRITION INFORMATION PER SERVING:

Calories: 162

Fat: 13.1g

Carbohydrates: 10g

Protein: 5g

8. In a bowl, add the flour, baking soda, and salt and mix well.
9. In another bowl, add the remaining Yacon syrup, coconut oil, eggs, and vanilla extract, and with a hand mixer, beat until well combined.
10. Add the flour mixture and beat until well combined.
11. Gently, fold in the candied bacon and chocolate chips.
12. With a tablespoon, place the balls onto the prepared cookie sheet in a single layer about two inches apart.
13. With your palm, flatten each ball slightly.
14. Bake for about 15 minutes or until the edges become golden brown.
15. Remove from the oven and place onto a wire rack to cool in the pan for about 5-10 minutes.
16. Carefully, invert the cookies onto the wire rack to cool completely before serving.

CHOCOLATE COOKIES

YIELD:

12 Servings

PREPARATION TIME:

15 Minutes

COOKING TIME:

12 Minutes

NUTRITION INFORMATION PER SERVING:

Calories: 35

Fat: 2.9g

Carbohydrates: 2.7g

Protein: 2.4g

INGREDIENTS:
- 2 large organic eggs
- 1 1/2 cups almond butter
- 2/3 cup cacao powder
- 1/3 cup powdered Erythritol
- 1/4 teaspoon salt

DIRECTIONS:
1. Preheat the oven to 320 degrees F. Line a large cookie sheet with parchment paper.
2. In a food processor, add all of the ingredients and pulse until a dough forms.
3. Make twelve equal-sized balls from dough and place onto the prepared cookie sheet in a single layer about two inches apart.
4. With your palm, flatten each ball slightly.
5. Bake for about 12 minutes or until the edges become golden brown.
6. Remove from the oven and place onto a wire rack to cool in the pan for about 5-10 minutes.
7. Carefully, invert the cookies onto the wire rack to cool completely before serving.

DOUBLE CHOC- OLATE COOKIES

YIELD:

18 Servings

PREPARATION TIME:

15 Minutes

COOKING TIME:

11 Minutes

INGREDIENTS:
- 2 large organic eggs
- 1 cup natural creamy almond butter
- 2 tablespoons peanut butter
- 1 tablespoon salted butter, melted
- 2/3 cup powdered Erythritol
- 2 tablespoons cacao powder
- 1 teaspoon baking soda
- 2 tablespoons water
- 1 1/2 teaspoons organic vanilla extract
- 1/4 cup 70% dark chocolate chips

DIRECTIONS:
1. Preheat the oven to 350 degrees F. Line a large cookie sheet with parchment paper.
2. In a large bowl, add all of the ingredients except the chocolate chips, and with an electric hand mixer, mix until well combined.
3. Fold in the chocolate chips.
4. Make about 1 1/2-inch balls from the dough and place onto the prepared cookie sheet in a single layer about two inches apart.
5. With your palm, flatten each ball slightly.

NUTRITION INFORMATION PER SERVING:

Calories: 40

Fat: 3.2g

Carbohydrates: 2g

Protein: 1.6g

6. Bake for about 8-11 minutes or until the edges become golden brown.
7. Remove from the oven and place onto a wire rack to cool in the pan for about 5-10 minutes.
8. Carefully, invert the cookies onto the wire rack to cool completely before serving.

YIELD:

PREPARATION TIME:

COOKING TIME:

NUTRITION INFORMATION PER SERVING:

Calories: 174

Fat: 14.4g

Carbohydrates: 7.8g

Protein: 5g

CHOCO- LATE KISS COOKIES

INGREDIENTS:
FOR COOKIES:
- 1 1/2 cups peanut flour
- 1 cup almond flour
- 3 tablespoons coconut flour
- 1 teaspoon organic baking powder
- 1/2 teaspoon salt
- 1 cup Swerve Sweetener
- 1 cup creamy peanut butter
- 3/4 cup butter, softened
- 2 organic eggs
- 1 teaspoon organic vanilla extract
- 1/4 cup powdered Swerve

FOR CHOCOLATE KISSES:
- 6 ounces 70% dark chocolate, chopped
- 2 tablespoons butter

DIRECTIONS:
1. Preheat the oven to 325 degrees F. Line two to three cookie sheets with parchment paper.
2. For cookies: in a bowl, add the flours, baking powder, and salt and mix well.
3. In another large bowl, add the Swerve, peanut butter, and butter and beat until creamy.
4. Add the eggs and vanilla extract and beat until well combined.
5. Add the flour mixture and mix until dough comes together.

6. Make one-inch balls from the dough and place onto the prepared cookie sheet in a single layer about two inches apart.
7. With your palm, flatten each ball slightly.
8. With your thumb, press an indentation in the center of each cookie.
9. Bake for about 15 minutes or until the edges become golden brown.
10. Remove from the oven and sprinkle with powdered Swerve.
11. Place the cookie sheets onto a wire rack to cool in the pans for about 5-10 minutes.
12. For the chocolate kisses: in a microwave-safe bowl, add the chocolate and butter and microwave until melted completely.
13. Stir well and set aside to cool until thickened.
14. Carefully, invert the cookies onto the wire rack.
15. Place a dollop into the well of each cookie and set aside for about 1 hour before serving.

THUMBPRINT COOKIES

YIELD:

20 Servings

PREPARATION TIME:

20 Minutes

COOKING TIME:

15 Minutes

INGREDIENTS:
- 2 ounces unsalted butter, softened
- 2 ounces full-fat cream cheese, softened
- 5 tablespoons granulated Erythritol
- 1/2 teaspoon organic vanilla extract
- 1 organic medium egg
- 1 1/2 cups almond flour
- 1 ounce sugar-free raspberry jam

DIRECTIONS:
1. Preheat the oven to 350 degrees F. Line a large cookie sheet with parchment paper.
2. In a bowl, add the butter, cream cheese, Erythritol, and vanilla extract, and with a hand blender, beat until smooth.
3. Add the egg and beat until well combined.
4. Add the almond flour and mix until well combined.
5. Make small equal-sized balls from the dough and place onto the prepared cookie sheet in a single layer about two inches apart.
6. With your palm, flatten each ball slightly.
7. With your thumb, press an indentation in the center of each cookie.
8. Fill indentation of each cookie with the raspberry jam

NUTRITION INFORMATION PER SERVING:

Calories:	86
Fat:	7.7g
Carbohydrates:	3.1g
Protein:	2.3g

9. Bake for about 15 minutes or until the edges become golden brown.
10. Remove from the oven and place onto a wire rack to cool in the pan for about 5-10 minutes.
11. Carefully, invert the cookies onto the wire rack to cool completely before serving.

MERINGUE COOKIES

YIELD: 18 Servings

PREPARATION TIME: 15 Minutes

COOKING TIME: 40 Minutes

INGREDIENTS:
- 4 large organic egg whites
- 1/4 teaspoon cream of tartar
- 6 tablespoons powdered Swerve, divided
- 1/3 teaspoon almond extract
- Pinch of salt

DIRECTIONS:
1. Preheat the oven to 210 degrees F. Line two to three baking sheets with parchment paper.
2. In a bowl, add egg whites and the cream of tartar, and with an electric mixer, beat on medium speed until frothy.
3. Add three tablespoons of Swerve, the almond extract, and the salt and beat on high speed until the egg whites are whipped into a medium consistency.
4. Add the remaining Swerve and beat on high speed until very stiff.
5. Scrape the meringue and beat until well combined.
6. Transfer the meringue into a piping bag, fitted with a large star-shaped tip and pipe rosette shape cookies onto the prepared baking sheets.
7. Bake for about 40 minutes.

NUTRITION INFORMATION PER SERVING:

Calories: 6

Fat: 0g

Carbohydrates: .8g

Protein: .8g

8. Turn the oven off but keep the baking sheets in the oven for about 1 hour with a little door opened.
9. Remove from oven and put the cookie sheet onto a wire rack for about 30 minutes before serving.

CREAM CHEESE COOKIES

YIELD:

24 Servings

PREPARATION TIME:

15 Minutes

COOKING TIME:

15 Minutes

NUTRITION INFORMATION PER SERVING:

Calories: 111

Fat: 9.4g

Carbohydrates: 3.1g

Protein: 3.4g

INGREDIENTS:
- 3 cups almond flour
- 1/4 teaspoon salt
- 1/2 cup Erythritol
- 2 ounces cream cheese, softened
- 1/4 cup butter, softened
- 1 large organic egg white
- 2 teaspoons organic vanilla extract

DIRECTIONS:
1. Preheat the oven to 350 degrees F. Line a larger cookie sheet with parchment paper.
2. In a bowl, add flour and salt and mix well.
3. In the bowl of a stand mixer, add the Erythritol, cream cheese, and butter and mix until fluffy and light.
4. Add the egg white and vanilla extract and mix until well combined.
5. Slowly, add flour mixture, 1/2 cup at a time, and beat until a little crumbly dough forms.
6. With a medium cookie scoop, place the mixture onto the prepared baking sheet about one inch apart, and with your hand, flatten each cookie slightly.

7. Bake for about 15 minutes or until the edges become golden brown.
8. Remove from the oven and place onto a wire rack to cool in the pan for about 5-10 minutes.
9. Carefully, invert the cookies onto the wire rack to cool completely before serving.

CREAM CHEESE PUMPKIN COOKIES

YIELD:

16 Servings

PREPARATION TIME:

15 Minutes

COOKING TIME:

25 Minutes

NUTRITION INFORMATION PER SERVING:

Calories: 75

Fat: 7.7g

Carbohydrates: 1.2g

Protein: 0.6g

INGREDIENTS:
- 1/2 cup coconut flour
- 1 1/2 teaspoons pumpkin pie spice
- 1/4 teaspoon salt
- 1/2 cup Erythritol
- 1/2 cup unsalted butter, softened
- 3 ounces cream cheese, softened
- 1/2 cup homemade pumpkin puree
- 1 teaspoon organic vanilla extract

DIRECTIONS:
1. Preheat the oven to 350 degrees F. Line a large cookie sheet with parchment paper.
2. In a bowl, add the flour, pumpkin pie spice, and salt and mix well.
3. In another bowl, add the butter and Erythritol and beat until creamy.
4. Add the cream cheese, pumpkin puree, and vanilla extra and beat until smooth.
5. Add the flour mixture and beat until combined.
6. Make small equal-sized balls from the dough.
7. Place the dough balls onto the prepared cookie sheet in a single layer about two inches apart.

8. With your palm, flatten each ball slightly.
9. Bake for about 25 minutes or until the edges become golden brown.
10. Remove from the oven and place onto a wire rack to cool in the pan for about 5-10 minutes.
11. Carefully, invert the cookies onto the wire rack to cool completely before serving.

ORANGE CREAM CHEESE COOKIES

YIELD:

15 Servings

PREPARATION TIME:

20 Minutes

COOKING TIME:

12 Minutes

INGREDIENTS:
- 1 cup almond flour
- 1/4 cup coconut flour
- 1 teaspoon organic baking powder
- 1 teaspoon ground cardamom
- 1/2 teaspoon ground ginger
- 1/2 cup Swerve sweetener
- 1/2 cup cream cheese, softened
- 1/2 cup butter, softened
- 1 organic egg
- 1 orange, zested finely
- 1 teaspoon organic vanilla extract

NUTRITION INFORMATION PER SERVING:

Calories: 131

Fat: 12.9g

Carbohydrates: 2.4g

Protein: 2.7g

DIRECTIONS:
1. In a bowl, add the flours, baking powder, and spices and mix well.
2. In another bowl, add the Swerve, cream cheese, and butter and beat until light and fluffy.
3. Add the egg, orange zest, and vanilla extract and beat until well combined.
4. Add the flour mixture and mix until well combined.
5. With parchment paper, cover the dough and refrigerate for at least 1 hour.

6. Preheat the oven to 350 degrees F. Line a large cookie sheet with parchment paper.
7. Remove from the refrigerator and make fifteen equal-sized balls from the dough.
8. Place the balls onto the prepared cookie sheet in a single layer about two inches apart, and with your palm, flatten each ball slightly.
9. Bake for about 10-12 minutes or until the edges become golden brown.
10. Remove from the oven and place onto a wire rack to cool in the pan for about 5-10 minutes.
11. Carefully, invert the cookies onto the wire rack to cool completely before serving.

CHOCOLATE SANDWICH COOKIES

YIELD:

6 Servings

PREPARATION TIME:

20 Minutes

COOKING TIME:

9 Minutes

NUTRITION INFORMATION PER SERVING:

Calories: 297

Fat: 27.1g

Carbohydrates: 5.2g

Protein: 10.8g

INGREDIENTS:
FOR COOKIES:
- 1/2 cup coconut flour
- 1/4 cup cacao powder
- 1/4 cup granulated Erythritol
- 3/4 teaspoon organic baking powder
- 1/8 teaspoon salt
- 4 large organic eggs
- 1/4 cup unsweetened almond milk
- 1/4 cup coconut oil, melted
- 1 teaspoon organic vanilla extract
- 1/2 teaspoon liquid stevia

FOR FROSTING:
- 8 ounces cream cheese, softened
- 6 ounces plain fat-free Greek yogurt
- 2/3 cup powdered Erythritol
- 1 teaspoon organic vanilla extract

DIRECTIONS:
1. Preheat the oven to 350 degrees F. Line two large cookie sheets with parchment paper.
2. In a bowl, sift together the coconut flour, cocoa powder, Erythritol, baking powder, and salt and mix well.

3. In another large bowl, add the eggs, almond milk, coconut oil, vanilla extract, and stevia and beat until well combined.
4. Add the flour mixture and mix until well combined.
5. With a cookie scooper, place twelve cookies onto the prepared cookie sheet in a single layer about two inches apart.
6. Bake for about 9 minutes or until the edges become golden brown.
7. Remove from the oven and place onto a wire rack to cool in the pan for about 5-10 minutes.
8. Carefully, invert the cookies onto the wire rack to cool completely before frosting.
9. For frosting: in the bowl of an electric stand mixer, fitted with a whisk attachment, add all of the ingredients and mix on high speed until smooth.
10. Place six cookies onto a smooth surface.
11. Place a thick layer of frosting over each cookie evenly.
12. Top with remaining cookies to make a sandwich and serve.

PUMPKIN SANDWICH COOKIES

YIELD:

6 Servings

PREPARATION TIME:

20 Minutes

COOKING TIME:

22 Minutes

NUTRITION INFORMATION PER SERVING:

Calories: 427

Fat: 32.8g

Carbohydrates: 3g

Protein: 29g

INGREDIENTS:
FOR COOKIES:
- 2 cups almond flour
- 1/2 cup Swerve Sweetener
- 1/2 teaspoon baking soda
- 1/4 teaspoon organic baking powder
- 1 1/2 teaspoons pumpkin pie spice
- 1/2 teaspoon salt
- 2 tablespoons coconut oil, melted
- 1/3 cup homemade pumpkin puree
- 1/4 cup unsweetened almond milk
- 2 large organic eggs
- 1 tablespoon organic vanilla extract

FOR FROSTING:
- 8 ounces cream cheese, softened
- 4 tablespoons butter, softened
- 1/4 cup Swerve Sweetener
- 1 teaspoon organic vanilla extract
- 1/3 cup heavy cream

FOR SPRINKLING:
- 1 tablespoon powdered Erythritol

DIRECTIONS:
1. Preheat the oven to 350 degrees F. Line two large cookie sheets with parchment paper.

2. For cookies: in a bowl, sift together the flour, Erythritol, baking soda, baking powder, pumpkin pie spice, and salt.
3. Add the coconut oil and beat until well combined.
4. In another bowl, add the pumpkin puree, almond milk, eggs, and vanilla extract and beat until well combined.
5. Add the flour mixture and mix until well combined.
6. Place about twelve cookies onto the prepared cookie sheets in a single layer about two inches apart.
7. With your palm, flatten each cookie slightly.
8. Bake for about 18-22 minutes or until the edges become golden brown.
9. Remove from the oven and place onto a wire rack to cool in the pan for about 5-10 minutes.
10. Carefully, invert the cookies onto the wire rack to cool completely before frosting.
11. For frosting: in a bowl, add the cream cheese and butter and beat until smooth and fluffy.
12. Add the Erythritol and vanilla extract and beat until well combined.
13. In another bowl, add the cream and beat until stiff peaks form.
14. Fold about 1/3 of the whipped cream into the cream cheese mixture.
15. Gently, fold in the remaining whipped cream.
16. Place six cookies onto a smooth surface.
17. Place a thick layer of frosting over each cookie evenly.
18. Top with remaining cookies to make a sandwich.
19. Sprinkle with the powdered Erythritol and serve.

Printed in Great Britain
by Amazon